W9-BXL-571

Designed by Flowerpot Press
www.FlowerpotPress.com
CHC-0909-0515
ISBN: 978-1-4867-2073-6
Made in China/Fabriqué en Chine

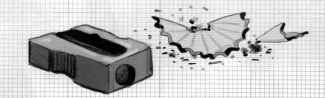

HOW DOES SOAP CLEAN YOUR HANDS?

THE SCIENCE BEHIND HEALTHY HABITS

written by madeline j. hayes

illustrated by srimalie bassani

How do you do all the things that you do? How do you think and breathe and live? Your body does it all for you!

The human body is amazing! It can fight off diseases, turn food into energy, and keep you safe so you can go out and explore the world. Your body does so many wonderful things all on its own without you even realizing it, but there are also a number of things you can do to help your body stay healthy. By giving your body the right nutrients, taking precautions to keep from getting sick, and giving yourself the rest and physical activity your body needs, you can help make yourself stronger, healthier, and happier. Learn more about some of these healthy habits and how you can use them to keep your body in tip-top shape!

Plenty of Sleep = A Super Brain

How does soap clean your hands?

Is there a soap squad of bubble buddies that pick up dirt and germs and carry them away?

Soap squad? Bubble buddies? No way! Well, kind of...

We all know we're supposed to wash our hands to keep us healthy, but why? What does the soap actually do? Lots of people think soap kills the germs and bacteria that build up on your hands. But actually, soap and water help move the germs and bacteria off of your hands and into the sink.

Soap does this by surrounding the germs and bacteria like a protective bubble and moving them with the water running off of your hands. Sometimes soap has added antibacterial products that help target and kill the bacteria on your hands and body, but that only adds to the work already being done by the soap. Antibacterial soap and regular soap are both about equally effective when it comes to cleaning your hands.

Soap and water put in a lot of work to keep you healthy, but you can help them out by following these steps.

1. Always wash your hands when they are dirty. It's especially important after you sneeze, cough, blow your nose, use the restroom, pet or touch an animal, before you eat, and if you are sick.

2. Wash your hands right before you interact with someone considered at risk. This includes children and babies, elderly people, and people who are sick or have conditions that make it hard for them to fight illnesses.

3. Wash your whole hand—even underneath your fingernails. Germs can hide anywhere, so make sure you're tracking them down with soap.

SOAP

If you sing the "Happy Birthday" song twice, you'll know you've washed your hands for the right amount of time.

4. Always wash your hands for 20 to 30 seconds. An easy way to do this is by singing a song or counting in your head.

5. If you can't wash your hands, avoid touching your eyes, nose, and mouth. Germs are most dangerous when they get inside your body!

Happy birthday to you! Happy birthday to you! Happy birthday to you! Happy birthday...

How does covering your cough help your neighbors?

Does it just make them happy to see you do a dab?
Maybe...but that's not what really helps them.

BAD VIRUSES!

Exit

Enter

The best way to protect yourself and your friends is to always cough or sneeze into a tissue, immediately throw it away, and wash your hands before you touch anything else. If you don't have a tissue, cough or sneeze into the crook of your elbow and be sure that your elbow is pointed toward the ground, kind of like you're doing a dab! We do these things to help slow the spread of a virus.

Cough

Cough

Sneeze

Sneeze

Do The Dab

Viruses infect cells and spread quickly by taking over the cells of living organisms. The cells the virus takes over are called host cells and once the virus controls the host cells, they tell them to make more of the virus. Eventually, the host cells can build up so much virus that they begin to harm the organism they have infected. That's why if a virus is in your body, it usually causes you to feel sick.

Virus

Cell

Hand Sanitizer

The best way to fight a virus is to contain it, which means slowing or stopping the spread. To do this, we have to be careful about how we interact with each other when we are sick. If you are sick, you need to wash your hands A LOT, be careful when you cough and sneeze, and keep your distance from others, if possible.

How does medicine make you better?

Does it discuss your feelings with you and help you see the sunny side of life? That would be nice, but what medicine really does is fix the physical part of you that is sick or hurt.

Think of viruses as an army of little robots coming to attack your body. Your immune system is the superhero hiding inside you that will jump into action to protect you by fighting back on behalf of your healthy cells. Your body has a system of cells, tissues, and organs that recognize and attack infections, diseases, and parasites, and they do this without attacking healthy cells. Medicine helps the immune system with that fight.

Cough

Dab

Dab

Sneeze

If you sneeze, do the dab!

I don't feel well...

We're going to do our best to make you feel better!

Tissue

MEDICINE

Ways to help your immune system:

Walk

Play

Eat Healthy Food

Sleep

Drink Water

Many things affect how well your immune system functions. Some things you can control, like exercise, sleep, and good nutrition, and some you cannot, like your genetics, or the traits you are born with. This combination of different factors makes everybody's immune system unique.

Medicine helps your immune system fight diseases in a couple different ways.

Vaccines are a unique medicine because you get them before you have a disease. They stimulate your immune system to build up a resistance to the targeted disease or virus, so if you encounter it after you have received a vaccine, your body already has practice fighting it off.

Symptoms medications don't attack the disease or virus, instead they treat your symptoms, like a headache or fever, so that you don't feel as bad.

Treatment medication is targeted to cure you from your disease. These types of medications are not always available, but when they are, they usually work with your immune system to get rid of the virus that is causing you to feel sick.

How does healthy eating make your body stronger?

Is it all that exercise you get from lifting food to your mouth? Hmm... probably not!

Your body does a lot to keep you healthy, so it's important that you treat it well. It starts with what you feed it. Nutrients are what your body needs to keep working, growing, and maintaining your everyday functions and your immune system.
Nutrients are the gas that fuels your body.

There are all sorts of nutrients. Vitamins and healthy foods, like fruits and vegetables, give you healthier nutrients than things like hamburgers and pizza. That doesn't mean you can't eat hamburgers and pizza—they give you some nutrients too—it just means you should eat a well-balanced diet.

PROTEIN

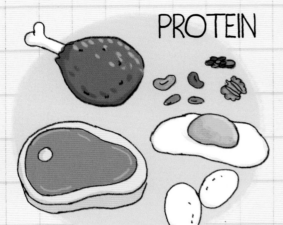

Protein helps your body grow and stay strong. You can get protein from meat, nuts, and eggs.

FATS

Fats help protect your body and help you absorb and use other types of nutrients. You can get fats from oils, butter, meat, and fish.

CARBOHYDRATES

Carbohydrates fuel your body, especially your brain, and help protect it against diseases. You can get carbohydrates from bread, pasta, cereal, potatoes, and beans.

VITAMINS

Vitamins are great for staying healthy. More vitamins tend to mean better skin, better vision, and stronger bones! You can get vitamins from fruits and vegetables.

MINERALS

Minerals help strengthen your bones and teeth. They also help turn food into energy, putting all these nutrients to good use. You can find minerals in all types of food.

CEREAL

WATER

Water is essential to your body. It helps your brain work better by flushing out toxins. Make sure you drink lots of water!

How does exercise make you less tired?

Do you get to take a nap while you exercise? Well maybe in Savasana, if your exercise is yoga, but usually that is not the case.

I call this nap pose!

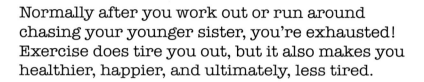

Normally after you work out or run around chasing your younger sister, you're exhausted! Exercise does tire you out, but it also makes you healthier, happier, and ultimately, less tired.

Your body is smart and if you train it, it will learn. Exercise and movement help to strengthen your heart, lungs, bones, and muscles. Over time they respond by building themselves up. Your body uses resources it doesn't need, like unhealthy fats, to fuel resources it does need, like muscles. Having a stronger, healthier body from exercise means you are less tired as you go about your day.

I love nap pose!

Regular exercise strengthens your heart. When you are moving, your heart beats faster to keep up with you. A stronger heartbeat leads to more blood moving throughout your body faster. Your blood carries oxygen, which is what you breathe. When your blood flow increases, the oxygen levels in your body also increase. More oxygen allows your muscles to recover faster and helps you feel less tired.

TIME FOR FITNESS

Sweating while exercising is also good for you. Your body sweats to help keep your body temperature where it needs to be, so you don't overheat. You need to make sure you're drinking lots of water to replace all the water you lose when you sweat.

Finally, exercise improves your mood, which is the best perk of all! Exercise releases natural endorphins in your body. Endorphins make you feel good. Exercise tells your body to send happy signals to your brain. It may not always be easy when you are doing it, but over time, your body adjusts and you will be more awake and happy when you exercise.

How does sleep make you healthier and smarter?

Do little elf librarians sneak into your room and read you books all night? Well that would be awesome if it were true, but unfortunately, that has never been proven.

Sleep is how you nourish your brain. Of course, your brain is part of your body and the food you eat will affect your brain, but the most important thing your brain needs is for you to sleep.

Sleep is like a pit stop for your brain as it races through life. Sleeping gives your brain a break from taking care of all the things your body does throughout the day, like walking, talking, reading, and playing, allowing it to reset. Scientists believe that while you sleep and dream, your brain is thinking, working, organizing, and building. The work your brain is doing while you sleep helps you remember things better. This is why it's so important to get a good night's sleep before a big test!

Sleeping also helps your mood and energy levels, which helps you focus, learn, and do more throughout the day. A well-rested brain running a well-nourished body has the power to fight intrusions when they occur.

Go Faster!

HOW SOAP REALLY WORKS

Soap is made up of two parts. One part is hydrophilic, which means it is pulled to interact with water.

HYDROPHILIC

The other part is hydrophobic, which means it is repelled by water and naturally moves away from it.

HYDROPHOBIC

Germs and bacteria are more appealing to the hydrophobic part of soap than the water. This means that the hydrophobic part of soap attracts the germs and dirt and arranges a bubble around them on your hands.

Once they are trapped in the bubble, they are washed away by the water.

TRY IT OUT

You can see how soap works using some things you can find around your home.

What you need:

- a plate or a bowl
- water
- black pepper
- dishwashing liquid

How it works:

1. Add the water to a plate or a bowl. You only need enough to just cover the bottom of the plate or bowl.

2. Shake some pepper onto the water's surface. Use enough pepper so the surface of the water is covered.

3. Dip your finger into the water. Note that nothing really changes in the water.

4. Now dip your finger into the dishwashing liquid. Once your finger is coated, place it in the water. The pepper should move away from your finger and to the outer edges of the bowl or plate.

This is a great way to see how the hydrophobic side of soap interacts with the water. When you add the dishwashing liquid to the water using your finger, the pepper shows you how the water reacts. This is similar to how soap moves the germs and bacteria from your hands by repelling the water.

FOOD FOR THOUGHT

As you know, nutrition is important in keeping your body strong and healthy. Look at the plate below and read the tips to learn what a balanced meal can look like and to find out more about how to give your body the nutrients it needs.

Grains: Grains are important and should take up about a fourth of your plate. Most of your grains should be whole, like whole-grain pasta, whole-wheat bread, and brown rice.

Protein: Protein should make up about a fourth of your plate. Healthy protein can come in the form of fish, beans, nuts, or poultry.

Fruits and Veggies: Half of your plate should be made up of fruits and vegetables. Try new ways to eat your veggies (raw or cooked) and periodically vary which ones you have. And remember that any fruit counts, so frozen fruit or 100% juice are also great ways to get what your body needs.

You can use this as a helpful guide, but also know that your plate can be modified in whatever way works best for you!

Water and Dairy: You should have about 5 to 8 glasses of water a day and roughly 2.5 to 3 cups of dairy. Dairy can be milk or even yogurt.

MAKE YOUR OWN HEALTHY SMOOTHIE USING SOME DELICIOUS FRUIT

Orange Smoothie Recipe

Packed full of vitamin C, this smoothie will bring some sunshine to your day!

Serving Size

2

Ingredients

1 cup orange juice
1 cup plain yogurt or milk of choice
1 tsp vanilla extract
1 orange, peeled
1 banana, peeled
1 cup ice

Directions

1. ASK AN ADULT to help you add orange juice, yogurt, and vanilla extract to a blender. Add the orange and banana to the blender and pour in the ice. Secure the blender lid and blend on high until smooth, about 1 minute.

2. Serve immediately or store covered in the refrigerator for up to 1 day.

GLOSSARY

Antibacterial – something that stops or slows the growth of bacteria

Bacteria – a group of tiny, single-celled organisms that can sometimes cause diseases

Cell – a small part in an organism's body that makes up tissues and organs

Cold – a common viral disease that affects the nose and throat, potentially resulting in a sore throat, a runny nose, and a lower body temperature

Coronavirus – a type of virus that can cause respiratory issues and symptoms such as shortness of breath, cough, and fever, like with COVID-19

Disease – something that affects the body and makes it harder for it to function correctly

Endorphins – hormones that come from the brain and are sent to the nervous system to make you feel better after certain activities take place, like exercising

Exercise – the act of training muscles to become stronger over time through physical activity

Fever – a body state that often comes from having a disease; it is typically characterized by higher body temperature and a worsening of the senses

Flu – short for influenza, a viral infection that is very contagious; it typically involves sore muscles and a fever

Genetics – the traits living beings inherit from their parents

Germ - a microorganism that can cause diseases

Host Cell – a cell where a virus reproduces inside of a living being

Immune System – the group of cells, tissues, and organs that help stop diseases from entering the body

Medicine – a substance used to help fight diseases

Nutrient – a substance that helps your body grow and get stronger

Symptom – the way in which a disease impacts your body, like a headache or a fever

Temperature – how hot a living being's body is; the average temperature for humans is around 98°F/37°C

Vaccine – a special medicine designed to help people from getting sick before they come in contact with a disease

Virus – an infectious agent that can replicate inside the cells of living organisms and can cause diseases